I'M GLAD THERE ARE...

Stars and the Moon

By Tracey Turner

Illustrated by Fiona Powers

WINDMILL BOOKS

Published in 2025 by Windmill Books,
an Imprint of Rosen Publishing
2544 Clinton St.
Buffalo, NY 14224

First published in Great Britain in 2022 by The Watts Publishing Group

Credits
Design and project management: Raspberry Books
Art Direction: Sidonie Beresford-Browne
Design: Kathryn Davies
Illustration: Fiona Powers

Cataloging-in-Publication Data

Names: Turner, Tracey, author. | Powers, Fiona, illustrator.
Title: Stars and the moon / by Tracey Turner, illustrated by Fiona Powers.
Description: Buffalo, New York : Windmill Books, 2025. | Series: I'm glad there are... | Includes glossary and index.
Identifiers: ISBN 9781538396407 (pbk.) | ISBN 9781538396414 (library bound) | ISBN 9781538396421 (ebook)
Subjects: LCSH: Astronomy--Juvenile literature. | Moon--Juvenile literature. | Stars--Juvenile literature.
Classification: LCC QB46.T87 2025 | DDC 520--dc23

Printed in the United States of America
CPSIA Compliance Information: Batch #CSWM25: For Further Information contact Rosen Publishing at 1-800-237-9932

I'M GLAD THERE ARE...

Stars and the Moon

By Tracey Turner

Illustrated by Fiona Powers

WINDMILL BOOKS

Contents

I'M GLAD THERE IS THE Night Sky

There are so many amazing things to look at:

- We can see other planets at night, even without a telescope!
- Our beautiful moon shines with light reflected from the sun.
- We can even spot the International Space Station as it whizzes around our planet carrying astronauts.

Wait until it's dark on a clear night and go skywatching. There is so much to see and to think about! I love gazing at the sky at night.

The more I find out about space, the more I love it. And the more I want to go there – I would like to be an astronaut one day!

The light from our homes and other buildings can make it hard to see the stars. If you live in the countryside it's easier to see them.

I'M GLAD THERE ARE

Stars

...because they twinkle and make nighttime magical.

ALL STARS – like our sun – are giant balls of burning gas in space. They were made from clouds of dust and gas long ago. Other stars are much farther away than our sun. And stars aren't really star-shaped.

Long ago, people looked at the same stars we see today and made groups of them into patterns and pictures. The groups are called constellations, and they all have names.

Spotting stars

When there's a dark night with no clouds, go star spotting with a grown-up. Can you see any of these constellations? They are named after characters from ancient Greek stories.

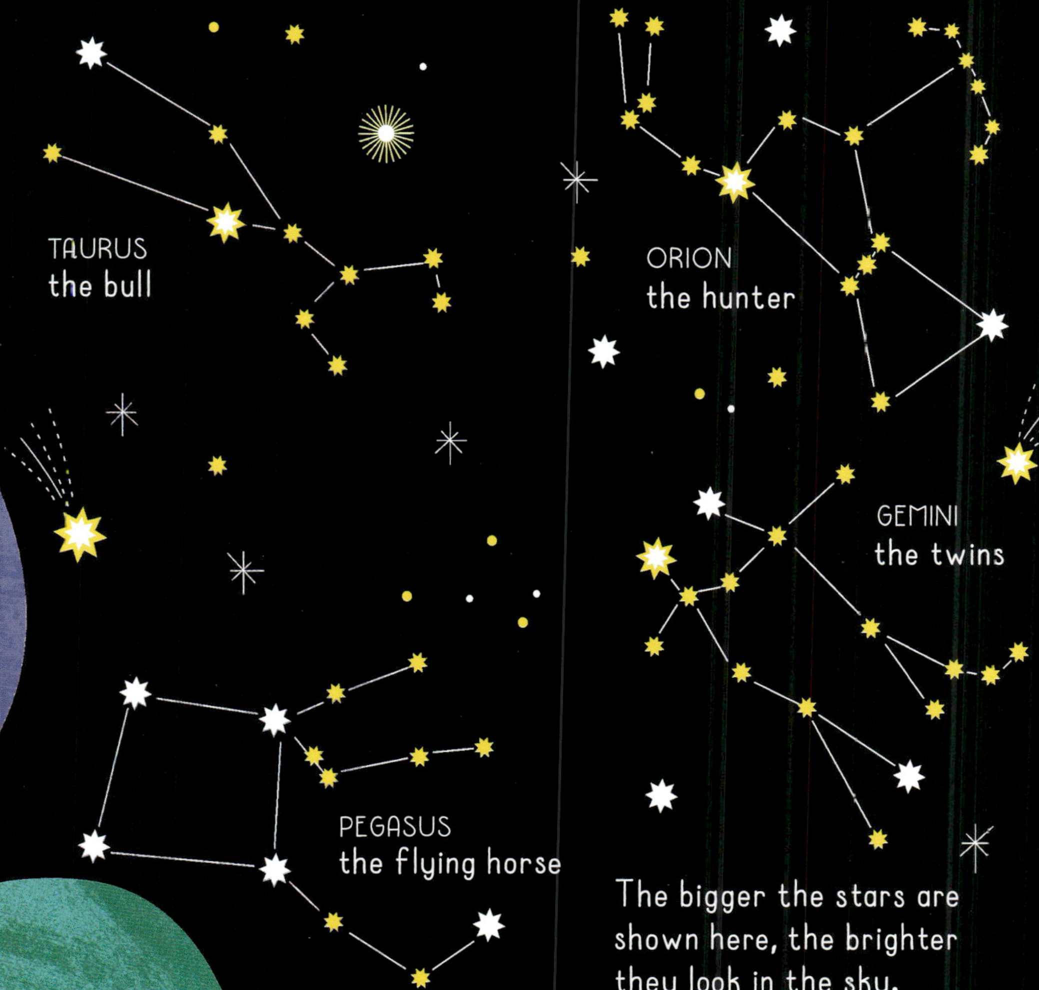

The bigger the stars are shown here, the brighter they look in the sky.

I'M GLAD THERE IS THE Moon

...because it's a beautiful glowing lantern in the sky.

The MOON is a ball of rock. It travels around Earth in a circle called an orbit.

Even though it sometimes seems to shine brightly, the moon doesn't have any light of its own. It glows with light reflected from the sun.

Sometimes we can see the whole moon – A FULL MOON.

Sometimes we can only see a little of one side – this is a CRESCENT MOON.

The moon takes a bit more than 27 days to travel around Earth. As it travels, it seems to change shape, because the sun shines on different parts of the moon as it makes its journey.

I'M GLAD THERE IS THE Sun

...because there wouldn't be any life without it.

The sun is a STAR. It's just the right distance away from planet Earth to give us warmth and light and help make plants grow.

NEVER LOOK DIRECTLY AT THE SUN! It can damage your eyes.

Earth travels around the sun. It takes one year for the Earth to go all the way around it.

The Earth spins as it travels around the sun. As it spins, some parts of the world face towards the sun while other parts are facing away from it.

This is what gives us night and day. When the sun is going down where you live, on the opposite side of the world the sun is coming up.

I'M GLAD THERE ARE Eclipses

...because they are spectacular and a bit spooky.

Sometimes the moon lines up directly with the sun during the day, casting a moon-shaped shadow on part of Earth below. Where the moon's shadow falls, it blocks out the sun's light and makes everything dark and eerie for a few minutes. This is called an ECLIPSE OF THE SUN or a SOLAR ECLIPSE.

Watch an eclipse only through special solar eclipse glasses – NEVER LOOK DIRECTLY AT THE ECLIPSE.

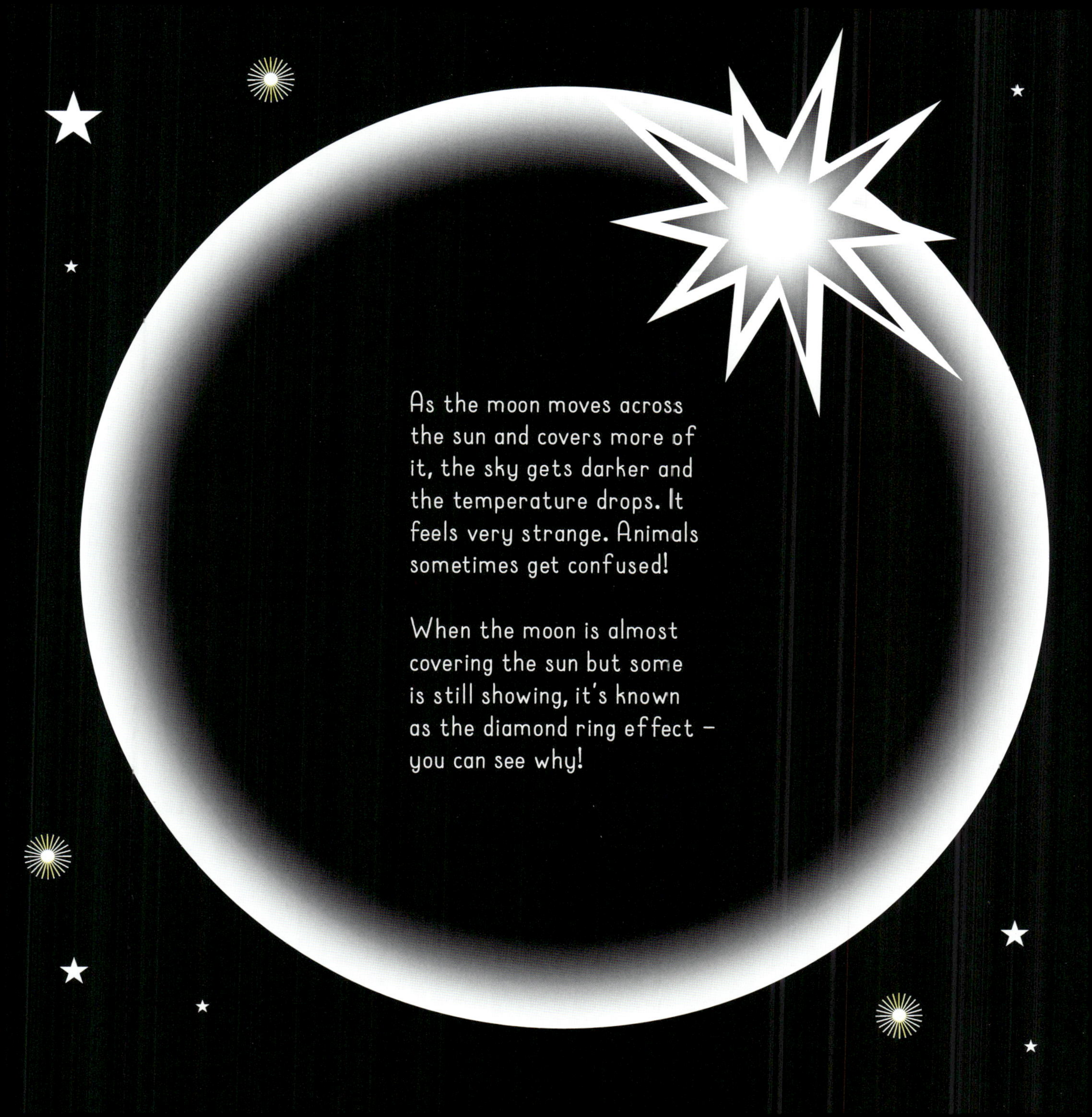

As the moon moves across the sun and covers more of it, the sky gets darker and the temperature drops. It feels very strange. Animals sometimes get confused!

When the moon is almost covering the sun but some is still showing, it's known as the diamond ring effect – you can see why!

I'M GLAD THAT Earth Is Tilted

...because it gives us seasons.

Earth spins around on a tilted axis. When it's summer where you live, your part of Earth is tilted towards the sun.

When it's winter where you live, your part of Earth is tilted away from the sun.

Not everywhere in the world has seasons. Near the equator – the imaginary line around the middle of Earth – it's hot all year round because it always gets direct light from the sun.

At the North Pole and the South Pole, the sun is always low in the sky. For half the year, the sun never rises and for the other half, the sun never sets!

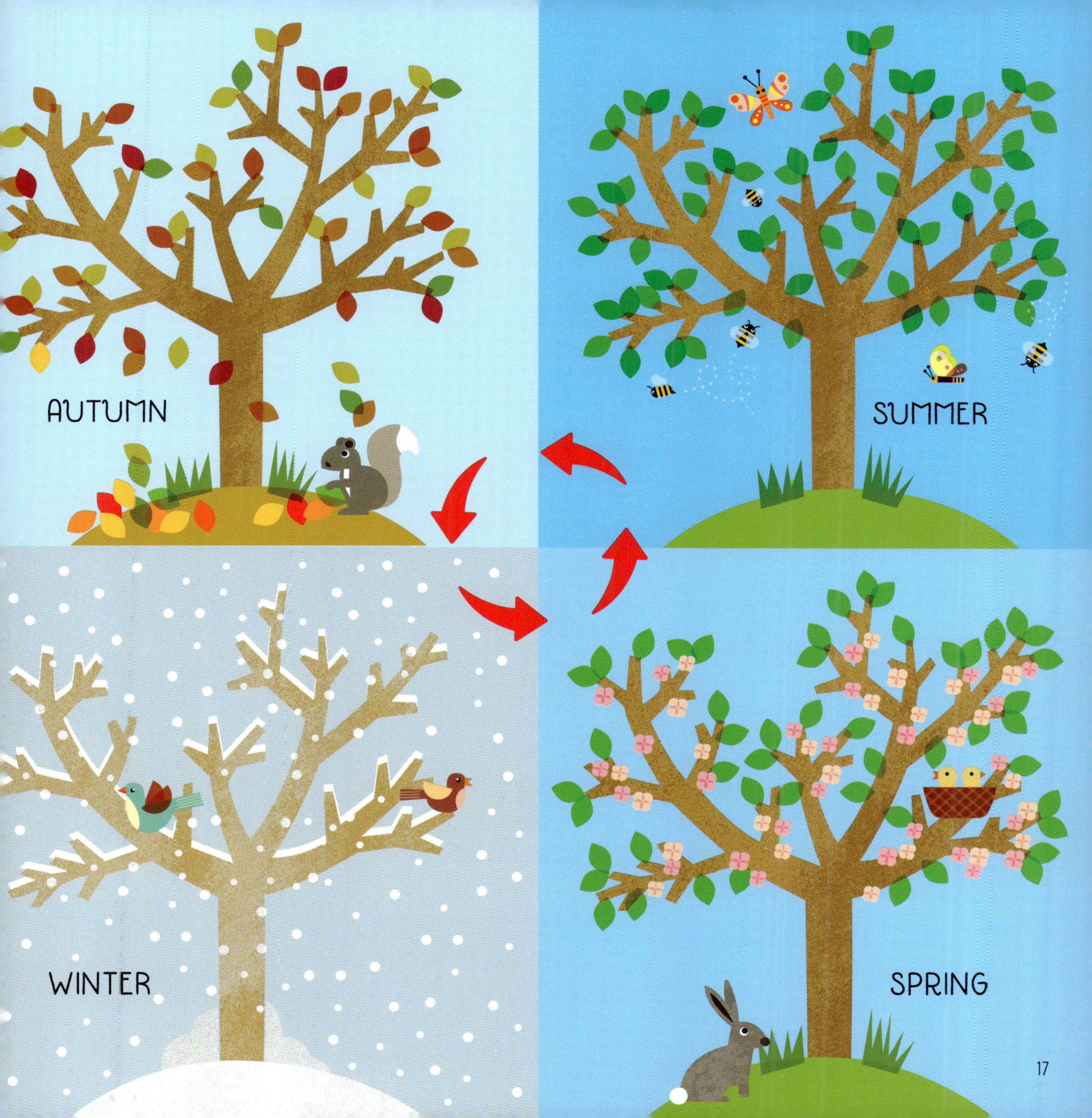
AUTUMN
SUMMER
WINTER
SPRING

I'M GLAD THERE IS A Solar System

...because there are whole other worlds we can see!

Earth is in orbit around the sun, along with other planets and asteroids. This is our **SOLAR SYSTEM.**

The three planets closest to Earth are Mercury, Venus, and Mars. Farther away, and much bigger, are Jupiter, Saturn, Neptune, and Uranus. Jupiter is so big you could fit all the other planets inside it!

Venus spotting

You can see some of the planets in the night sky using just your eyes. Venus is the easiest planet to spot. It's the brightest thing in the sky except for the moon. Find out when is the best time to look out for it where you live.

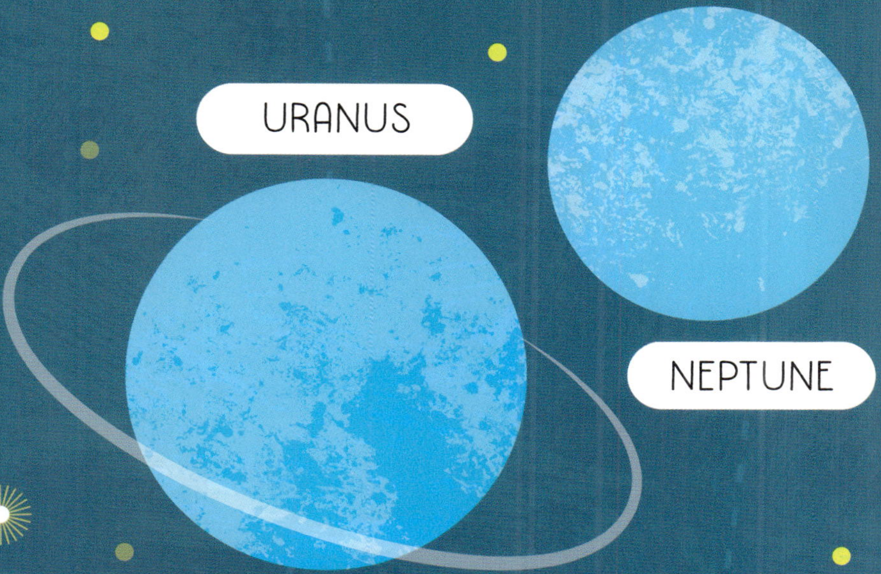

The sizes and distances are not to scale.

I'M GLAD THERE ARE

Shooting Stars

...because you can make a wish on them!

SHOOTING STARS aren't really stars at all. They are chunks of rock that have been floating around in space. Some of them reach Earth's atmosphere and hurtle towards the ground.

Some chunks of rock – called meteors – burn up in Earth's atmosphere. That's what makes the streak of light that you can sometimes see in the night sky. There's a legend that if you make a wish on a shooting star, the wish will come true!

Meteor showers

You might be lucky enough to see a meteor shower – lots of shooting stars streaking across the sky. Astronomers can predict meteor showers – find out if there might be one near you. Then ask a grown-up to take you meteor spotting!

I'M GLAD THERE ARE

Asteroids

...because they are spinning chunks of space rubble!

ASTEROIDS are bits of rock and metal. When the planets and moons in our solar system formed, the asteroids were the leftover bits and pieces.

In our solar system there's an asteroid belt – an enormous disc of rocks going around the sun between Mars and Jupiter. The biggest asteroid is a dwarf planet called Ceres.

MARS

Much farther away, there are more asteroids and comets in the Kuiper Belt, which is at least 20 times bigger than the asteroid belt.

Even though there are more than a million asteroids in the asteroid belt, it's so vast that there's lots of space between them. Spacecraft pass through with only a tiny chance of being hit.

I'M GLAD THERE IS THE

International Space Station

...because it's an awesome science lab in space!

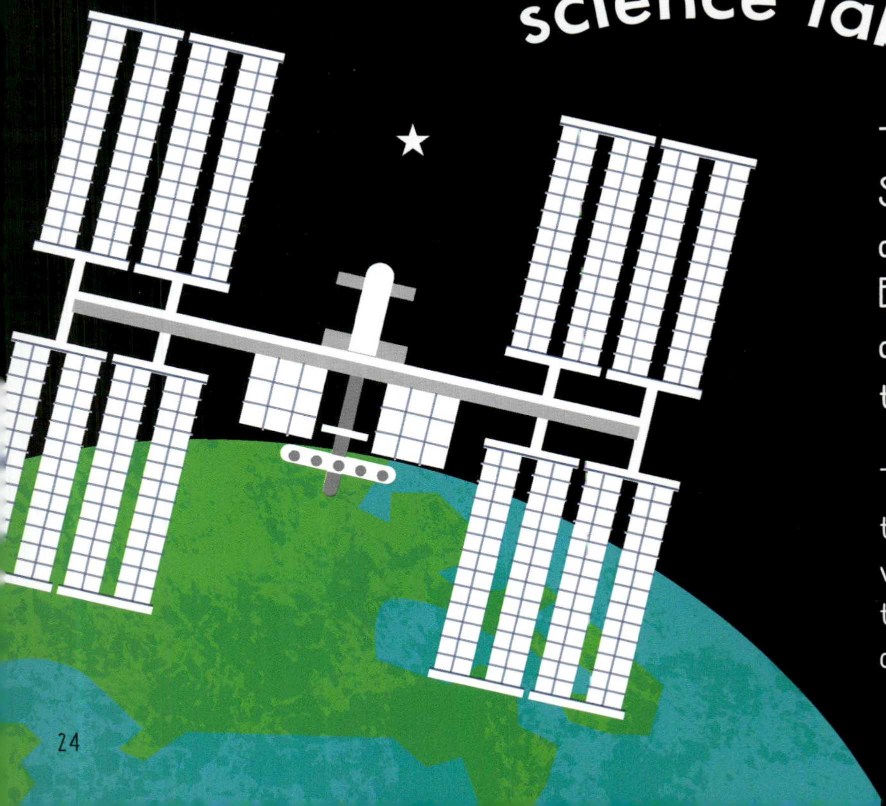

The International Space Station (ISS) is in orbit about 250 miles (400 km) above Earth. It takes an hour and a half for it to go all the way around Earth.

The astronauts who live aboard the ISS conduct experiments in very low gravity. They even study themselves, to see the effects of low gravity on their bodies.

Because of the low gravity, the astronauts float around everywhere! They have to learn how to wash, brush their teeth, go to the bathroom, and work while they're floating.

Astronauts on the ISS have come from all over the world. There are no arguments between countries – everyone works together. It's one of the reasons I think it's so awesome!

I'M GLAD THERE ARE

Astronauts and Rockets

...because they tell us more about the universe!

A ROCKET has to go very fast to get away from Earth's gravity – more than 24,800 miles per hour (40,000 km/h)! Rockets put satellites into orbit around Earth, or launch spacecraft on their journeys.

Satellites can take photos of space, gather information about Earth, or help people find their way and keep in touch.

Some spacecraft, such as the Mars rovers, land on other planets. They can send back pictures of themselves driving across the planet, and collect samples of its rocks and soil.

Sometimes rockets launch people into space – to get to the International Space Station, or even farther. The moon is the only place where people have set foot other than our own planet.

I'M GLAD THERE ARE

Galaxies

...because they make me think about how big and wonderful the universe is!

A GALAXY is a group of stars, gas, and dust that's all held together by gravity. Our own galaxy is called the Milky Way. From Earth, on a very dark, clear night, you can sometimes see our galaxy as a milky band of light.

The Milky Way is HUGE. Light moves so fast it could travel around the world in the blink of an eye. But it would take more than 100,000 years for light to travel across the Milky Way!

Our galaxy contains more than 100 billion stars. Who knows how many planets there might be in orbit around them? And it's just one of many, many galaxies in the universe.

YOU ARE HERE

GLOSSARY

Asteroid
a rocky object in space that orbits the sun.

Astronaut
someone trained to travel into space.

Astronomer
a scientist who studies space.

Atmosphere
the gases surrounding a planet.

Constellation
a group of stars that make up an imaginary picture.

Galaxy
a group of stars, planets, gas, and dust held together by gravity.

Legend
a traditional story from long ago.

Meteor
a piece of space rock that burns up in Earth's atmosphere, creating a streak of light.

Milky Way
our galaxy.

Moon
a natural object in orbit around a planet.

Not to scale
not representing accurate measurements.

Orbit
the path through space of a planet, moon, or star.

Planet
a large, round (or nearly round) object that orbits a star.

Rocket
a powerful spacecraft that launches satellites, astronauts, etc., into space.

Solar
to do with the sun.

Star
a ball of burning gas in space.

Sun
the star at the center of our solar system.

Telescope
a device we can look through that makes objects in the sky that are far away look closer.

Universe
all of space and everything within it.

INDEX